Just Yesterday
Poems From Another Life

Just Yesterday
Poems From Another Life

Kathleen E. Fearing

Book and cover design by
Kathleen E. Fearing

ISBN-13: 978-1502519313

Printed in the USA
G J Publishing
515 Cimarron Circle Suite 123
Loudon TN 37774
865-458-1355
www.neilans.com

Table of Contents

"It shocks me how I wish for ... what is lost
and cannot come back."
— Sue Monk Kidd

Just Yesterday

...the air crinkles
with laughter of children
that slips between
bristled hedges, hovers
like fireflies in thick evening air...
neighbors I've not met
and probably won't,
still I listen,
silent,
floating on the edges of
their smiles,
remembering my own
a thousand years ago,
or was it just yesterday
when everything was wrapped
in sureness and
magic was my secret name.

A Storm Rises

         …and, even though
crowds of
years have passed,
I am seven
again,
vulnerable – a moth trapped
in a storm –
hiding
under blankets,
covering
my ears
against
the howling
hurricane,
the cracking
branches…
doubting I
will survive such
unbridled
fury, yet,
all at once
alive, so
alive,
listening to my heart
beat in time
with each
gust of wind,
and I close
my eyes,
once more,
against the rage.

Bread

Saturday morning, elbows on the table, I
watch in awe as Mother stands – supreme
and gifted queen of all before her – and the
preparations commence: sifter sifts together
flour, baking powder, a pinch of salt;
elsewhere, eggs, warm milk, butter and
yeast melt into one silky smooth, aromatic
puddle; then in her earthen colored
crockery bowl – a light blue stripe
encircling its rim – Mother begins the
ancient, sacred ceremony: warm milk-
butter-yeast-egg mixture folded gently,
lovingly, into salt, flower and baking
powder, add some binding Quaker Oats;
then, those powerful hands mash together,
fold, mash, add more flour, mash, fold,
mash, until her well-trained eye, her
discerning fingers, know it's time.

The doughy blob is thrown down upon the
worn, faded metal top of the kitchen table –
transformed by a blizzard of King Arthur
flour; then – holding my breath, leaning
away slightly, every muscle poised for
what's to come – Mother plunges her great
Irish fist down into the warm, pliant mush,
folds it over, pushes, shoves her punishing
fist deep within the middle of its floured
softness, again and again, relentlessly
pounding, as though it had committed some
unspeakable crime.

3

Finally – its torture completed, gently
placed in the greased loaf pan – the fragrant
dough rests beneath a moist cloth in the
warm oven-womb where it rises to the
fullness of its promise, and baked until
brown; then – my patience rewarded –
Mother cuts me the first slice of homemade
oatmeal bread, covers it with sweet, melting
butter – indescribable ecstasy.
And all of life
is good.

Out of The Fire

...sunset
that dreamlike moment
when light surrenders
to all that is vague,
when shadows lay soft
against reality...

and I,
alone with
my paper and pen,
listen for
your footsteps
on my
darkened
path.

Hanging Flowers

Flowers,
      bought at their peak
      of flower perfection, then
      pushed into pots
          to thrive,
              or not,
seek t.l.c.,
a little water,
a daily clipping
of dead heads,
a loving hand, a
caring eye…

But some days
the caretaker
leaves the
potted blooms
to wither,
to cry
alone in aching
neglect,
when all they
wanted was
a touch of
      sweet
          water.

Cars

Outside my window
they blend
into the dull
hum of
another
afternoon…
      sometimes
           I wonder where
they go,
so fast,
looking neither
left nor right,
only straight ahead,
bullets into the
unknown,
as though
a lost love waits
      just
           out of sight…

Morning

Something sweet
blows through
the doorway of morning,
as though a special
perfume
is opened at
the rising of the sun and
explodes through
the new air,
perhaps
the essence of
leftover dreams
not quite gone,
savored,
held fast,
inhaled
one more time before
fading
into daylight.

Hours Later

The sweetness of blueberries
     from my summer harvest

lingers
     on my tongue,

and even tho
     they are gone,

I taste them,
     sweet   still,

like a promise,
     once so alive,

now,
     just a faded-cotton memory,

       …the blueberries
         of my summer.

Once Upon A Time

            …the world was
a magical place,
buttons were
real eyes,
uneven stitches across
a corduroy face smiled for
only me,
there was no
quiet hurt, no
empty glass,
but a soft touch to
beckon sleep,
a bewitching story to
lull away the small hurt
of the day…

            …when I loved
without thinking,
borrowed no time, and
savored each sweet
moment that passed my
open window.

Duke

The A Train
slips out of the station
pulling you and me
along its rhythmic journey
      come with me
            come with me
                  come with me
our feet
suspended in hot music
needing
to glimpse once more
a time lost to
time   a romance
forgotten
we reach for the brake to
slow the wheels
stop the momentum
savor a memory that
slips away with
the last
      pure note.

11

Gone

Trees
tugged by the wind
their leaves lost to the day
whisper to me
where
      where
             where
has time gone?

Same As Always

Flowers nod their summer heads,
        same as always.

Breeze filters thru drowsy maple leaves,
        as it will.

Sun heats my face.
Rain coats my skin,
        the same
                the same…

Yet –

Somewhere in the shadows
I hear
the lightness of
a young girl's
impulsive laughter,
nights expecting the right
to tomorrow,
days without lingering doubts
or the heavy dread that
I haven't done enough…

everything's the same
        everything's changed.

Shadows

Strips of darkness,
pinholes of light,
break through the
chair's webbing,
growing squares
of sunlight,
moving as the hour
advances,
exposing cracks
in my patio stones,
crevices which,
        when the sun hits at
            right
                 angles,
become canyons
where ants crawl
to hide away,
a safety zone of
quiet
darkness.

Storms Linger

...hang above my head
like noisy reminders of
powers far greater
than my will,

and who am I,
          after all,
but some airy
summer
seed to be
blown away
at the will of
          I know
                    not
                              what,
so far beyond what is understood,
the seed of life,
the echo in
a vast, lonely universe I try
to hear,
          but,
                    cannot.

Adrift

An unsuspecting dandelion seed
ripped from
its family, becomes
an aimless skiff upon a
sea of grass and clover,
until the breeze falters,
dropping the seed
where it will...
by accident
or fate,
its future connected now
to where it has landed,
to prosper or fail –

and I,
        adrift
over the dark, rude landscape,
        look to
where I would plant
my feet
        again.

Somehow

Somehow knowledge escapes
Somehow wisdom survives
What ray of sun would
Find you still there
Among the flower's petals
When so many had
Fallen away?

Peace

What tree,
strong, steadfast,
swirling in the thunder wind,
frozen to its spot,
yearning to grow,
what tree has not
made its peace
with the world?

And it all seems
so easy
from here,
to simply watch,
never understanding
the will,
the angry silent will
of a mighty oak,
to stretch
forever upward
toward the silver clouds,
thru the ever-thinning air,
seeking…

Silence

        …an absence of sound,
or perhaps
an invitation to
eavesdrop on the faint sighs
of birds,
the flutter of fireflies
on a ghost-pale night,
a gasp of perfection
thought   but not said,
beyond what the ear captures,
yet light on the soul,
forever lost in
the bark of a sound
that leaves me
starved.

Grace

And I thought,
if I take care of the flowers,
pull off the dead heads,
water and coo
at their sides,
reach my hands into
their soft, dark soil,
is there some grace
to be earned…
or is it
a way
to help me be
one more day?

Mariah
(The Wind)

       …rides on many faces,
spreads out
across seasons
and days,
both soft and
brutal,
tosses the birds,
like paper toys,
from the skies,
pushes storms out of sight
and drags them back again,
whistles thru drain pipes
to wander and rip the seas,
and in its wake,
I inhale
       its angry love.

Questions

The flowers are growing
better this year
and tho I ask them
they do not tell me
why…

Today

Things will happen,
they always do,
but not today
I think,
no,
today the sun warms
my cheeks,
the wind pushes
hair away
from my eyes,
like a mother
tending to her sleeping child,
bending to kiss away
all the bad.

Reservoir

A place where things
are stored,
a place I
fly,
mid night,
looking for
strength,
a deep well where
nothing, or everything,
lives, I either
drown in its depths,
or find a ladder
and climb out one
rung at a time,
a place I am
not sure exists,
until,
in desperate hours,
searching blindly,
I stretch my arms
into the void
hoping –
            hoping.

Sand Box

Sparrows hide
in the tall grass
between clover and
dandelions,
a reprieve from the world
of overbearing blue jays and crows;
then like children hiding in
the big kids' sandbox,
they sneak into the recesses of
my potted plants
whispering,
this is
mine,
      mine,
            mine.

A Place I Was

One quiet morning,
except for
the birds
      which, like rain splats on
      a tin roof,
      never stop their chatter…
the air was
thick with the white noise
of peace,
and time stopped
just briefly
enough
      to smell the heavy dust
         of yesterday,
            and remember.

Afternoon

The shoulders of the day
droop
in afternoon heat.

Sweat trickles down
its wide, sun-washed forehead.

Birds find a pool
to cool their feet.

A breeze drifts thru
lifting the heavy leaves.

All raise their heads
to capture the fleeting respite,
then,
          like a child's soft kiss,
                    it's gone.

Flower Petals

The soft pink petals
of impatiens
open to the sun –
      the rough, hot, hard sun –
still, they open,

forgiving,
      forgiving,
            wanting.

Cry of Birds

Before dawn
when time begins anew
and dreams
fade to gray
noise
the mournful doves
cry into that cool
mist of illusion
a fearful sound
echoing off the
dripping pines
seeps through closed doors
and deep into me
my eyes search
between the window blinds
for its source
making sure the cry
is not mine

Fog

Tongues of mist
lap at the morning river
tasting traces of fish,
there, and not;
the hysterical woodpecker cries
a heralding, or warning;
breeze stirs
the still-wet pines
bending toward
a new day
and what might be,
despite everything.

Crow Talk

Circling in
a constant, hard circle
high above the trees,
crows argue
some crow problem,
tossed about
from beak to beak,
insults
thrown at a
feral cat who,
unknowingly,
wanders into self-appointed
crow territory…
get out!
get out!
they cry;
but the cat ignores
their screeches
and walks her own way;
        this is my path
                my way,
for, what other
way can she travel
but her own?

Constrained

I am
      a dream in the night
I am
      a relentless yearning
I am
      a poem reaching
I am
      a wound healing
I am
      a deep well parched
I am
      an arrow searching
I am
      a wild animal wandering
I am
      an unheard river raging
I am
      woman
            head and
                  heart and
                        soul and

      constrained.

Leaves

      …stressed beyond endurance
by August heat,
      exhausted,
fall like lost dreams,
their lives shortened,
giving way to
the war nature wages on all her children,
surrendering to
that veil of tomorrow
through which we
cannot see.

Light

      ...plays tricks
with my eyes
leading me to think
I see
what I do not...
it's there,
it's gone,
a rabbit hole in time,
a trickster leaving only
an image
of what I thought
I saw,
or,
    what
        I hoped.

Once

      ...you said to me (or maybe it was
more than once)
don't cry
it does no good to cry.

Must I remember only that?
not a soft touch,
nor soothing words
after midnight dreams
that woke me sweating...

Must I remember only that?

The Tree

A storm came
it took down some trees
upturned them
their roots screaming into the air
no one could hear them
but the birds
whose homes once were there
in the now broken branches
other trees were
bent by the wind's hellish fury
limbs broken
then came the trucks
the workers
they sawed up the tree
damaged by the storm
they sawed it away
branch by broken branch
chewed it up
spit the bits into
a dump truck
yet, though her broken limbs were cut away
her beautiful shade gone
she refuses to die
a few resilient leaves
cling to her sides
and
the birds have come back

She

The way a branch bends
and then breaks
in an unforgiving wind,

the way the tide surrenders
to the moon's incessant pull,
she lent herself to

forces inside her slender mind,
mounting day by day,
like papers on a cluttered desk,

an uncontrollable wind,
an unrestrained
tide of doubt and

rambling hopelessness
that led finally to
her planned end…

how am I to understand,
how do I travel a different way
without knowing why,

without knowing?

A Sparrow

   ...its mouth full of dried weeds
plucked from my parched lawn,
looks again at my hanging pots
full of flowers,
to her, so full of promise,
and she,
like a storm driven by a furious wind,
would not be turned away,
tho' I tried to tell her
the bushes beyond the ditch
would be so much better,
back she came, and again,
shouted at me,
   I need a home
    for my babies,
and I wondered at
how well
this wild creature
cared for life
yet to come.

Midday Silence

...floats in aimless streams
across my backyard,
nestles like lazy fog between rocks in
my garden wall,
a silence rife with
cicada saws,
cardinal chirps,
wind tugging at
trees languid in late August sun;
and somewhere,
lost in the yawn of a summer afternoon,
the taut thread of yearning
lands at my feet
and waits.

Gone

Winter crawls, low,
into corners of the empty house –

      suspended ghostlike at the end
      of the narrow dirt road,

      like an old man
      waiting for his end –

deserted now of everything,
except hardscrabble memories –

      babies' cries,
      quiet sobbing behind
      closed doors,
      love's promise failed –

sighs drift in and out of
cracks in the walls…
no one hears them now,
except birds pausing for awhile to perch
on its fieldstone chimney,

a house alive only
in my half-sleep dreams

      and I awake
      gasping

        it's gone
           all gone.

Ocean Children

Waves lap against the shore,
              still, still,
and though
the laughing swimmers
have all gone,
         taken away
         by time and circumstance,
behind the pressed suits and
combed hair
they long to be
splashing,
splashing
in the salty, excited waves,
dodging crabs and jellyfish
like squares in a lost game of hopscotch,
searching for treasure
that spread out
before them
unseen,
unheard now,
except in those quiet times
when   in a vague dream
they stop
and listen
to the restless waves
inside.

Sweet Child

Running in fear
she coughs up
the dust of war
collecting in her lungs,
her heart
all but lost to the
world of hate;
and no end in sight.

August Wind

Soft, like threads of silk
against my skin,
the afternoon wind
blows a dream into me,
and caught within the white noise of
the wind's call,
I hear her song,
feel her
blistered hand,
weathered face,
skirts roughed by nagging squalls…
A Celtic soul who
lived and died beside
the sodden marsh,
the raging sea, and tho'
she walks beside me now in
the heady scent of an
August wind,
I cannot see her eyes.

Prayers

Riding on a Sunday morning
past green lawns,
past trees,
their branches bent low,
bowing to earth's divinity,
past churches
with their hunched over people
hoping for mercy,
a key to faith's favor.

Down along the river
with its quiet, flowing promise,
a profound silence sings
away the darkness
caused by those who *know*,
leaving a paradise,
a tribute unmatched
in any building.

Traces

And the
rains come,
like they do,
dripping
down,
smearing
the printed
page
where you
were written.

Locked Doors

There is something
saddening about
how we lock ourselves
away when the world
turns   when the
sun leaves the sky
and we say
let's go in, it's
getting dark,

for in that stunning
darkness –
          the animals know
          it well –
deep secrets are unveiled,
stars sing to the moon,
fireflies find their soul mates,
the owl on her branch
sees what we cannot…
          (do we try?)
and we,
locked behind
unyielding doors,
          miss it all.

Ireland

I don't want to talk about Ireland
about her wet green fields her fresh
salty morning air her music that
on the edge of life's night
fills my head and heart I don't want
to talk about the visions she's left
inside me the ones that bring tears
the ones of rosy-cheeked children of
old women in knotted scarves walking
with their heads low of pubs filled
to the brim with solid
hand-scarred farmers with long
sideburns smiling
living smoking drinking
laughing being Irish I don't want
to talk about her for I
cannot
be there.

Untouchable

Soft stars –
       untouchable wishes –
light my way –
       so easy to forget when
       day comes and they
       fade to another realm –
but tonight
I become
dance among
between
below
them
I am
a solitary line
shoelace shadow
on the moon-bleached dirt
exposed
bleeding-heart blushing
twirling in time with
heaven's
silent pulsars
lost in a space between
here
       and there.

Early Fall

Morning fog
that cold wet blanket of

time creeps into low spots
of my aging garden

mostly gone to seed now
still a lone purple cone flower

glows with a July barely
remembered dew hangs thick on

weeds more persistent than I
holding on to desire

lie down beside the last
daisies listening to their lament

weeping for one
more day of summer.

Books by Kathleen E. Fearing
All available at www.Amazon.com

Champ, A Race to Find The Truth,
  2010, 2014
Adisa's Basket, 2010
An Old Heart, Yesterday and Today,
  2010
*My Friend the Werewolf, What Would
  You Do?,* 2011
Women, Poems by Heart, 2011
*Mornings by the River, Poems in the
  Order of Things,* 2011
Voyage of Dreams, An Irish Memory,
  Celtic Cat Publishing,
  Knoxville, TN, 2012
*Caught in the Crossfire, Poems of Children
  in War,* 2013
My Story Time, 2013
Finding Hope, A Reason For Tomorrow,
  2014
Now and Then, Poems & Other Things
  2014
*The Night The Winds Came and Mama Sang
  Her Magic Song,* 2014

Kathleen E. Fearing has been writing stories for young people and poetry for adults for many years. She has published twelve books and is currently working on several others. Kathleen has an earned doctorate in education from the University of Massachusetts at Amherst, and has taught education, children's literature, and communications at the college level. She also has received several broadcasting awards for her children's radio programs.

Just Yesterday

Just Yesterday

15891102R00036

Made in the USA
Middletown, DE
26 November 2014